TRANSFORMATION BY TRADE

Achieving Lifelong Success Through Hands-On Learning

Jason Mullen

I dedicate this book to young people struggling with the idea of becoming successful and wondering about using the trades to achieve it.

Contents

With steady hands and focused eyes,
A craftsperson works where true skill lies.
Hammer to nail and saw to wood
Creating things for greater good.

In day's hard work,
They find their peace,
With every stroke,
Their skills increase.

In sweat and toil,
Their days unfold,
Crafting values
With hands that hold.

Not just a job, it's art you see,
In steel and wood, their canvas be,
Each crafted piece, a story told,
A testament to skills grown old.

Acknowledgements

I acknowledge my parents **Dan and Geraldine** for all their hard work which has rubbed off on me, making me a hard-worker, always allowing me to make my own decisions and mistakes, and enabling me to learn along the way.

I acknowledge my children **Meraina and Quin**, for making me the happiest dad. You both inspire me to keep improving myself. I hope to always make you proud to have me as your dad.

I acknowledge my sister **Karyn and her husband Raymond** for encouraging me to always keep learning. You have both supported me in every way over the years, specifically in getting this book done.

I acknowledge **Prashant Miranda** for being an inspiring friend. You are a man with the most beautiful soul. Thank you for creating my book cover.

I acknowledge my supporting friends **Wayne, Brad, and Kris**. I think of you as more than friends, but truly family.

I acknowledge **Donny Mac and Gerry Holley** who gave me my start in the trades. Thank you.

I acknowledge **Peel District School Board** for the opportunity to improve myself by starting as an electrician and graduating through several career promotions.

Foreword

As I read this book, I found myself stepping into the shoes of someone starting a fresh and exciting career path in the skilled trades. It's a hands-on journey where newcomers learn the ropes from experienced tradespeople, working step by step to build confidence and expertise.

What stands out in this book is the encouragement it will give you, urging you to see the bigger picture. It shows that with hard work, cooperation, and a keen attitude to learning, you can grow from a beginner into a respected and skilled professional.

What will really grab you about this story of life is the friendly hand Jason extends to you, inviting you to be a part of a community where people support each other, share knowledge, and work together to achieve common goals.

This is a warm and honest guide that inspires you to roll up your sleeves, learn a trade, and build a future full of opportunities, value, and success.

Raymond Aaron
New York Times **Bestselling Author**

Chapter 1

Decide

"The only way to do great work is to love what you do.
If you haven't found it yet, keep looking. Don't settle."
— Steve Jobs, Co-founder of Apple Inc.

1

Dreams Begin with a Thought

All dreams about your life begin with a thought. Picture in your mind a canvas, and you have the brush in your hand to paint the masterpiece of your life.

If you can imagine those dreams about your life becoming a reality, then the world is your playground. It's like sculpting a piece of art where you continuously mold yourself into the person of your dreams. Imagination is your golden ticket, a gateway to envision what those dreams look like, vivid and vibrant.

Dreams inspire you to break the norm, to tread a path less trodden. They empower you, whispering that you matter in this grand world, that you are not just another face in the crowd but somebody special, somebody with a unique story to tell.

Embracing Your Unique Vision

Remember, no one understands you or visualizes you the way you do yourself. No one can dive into the depths of your dreams like you can. The inner sanctum of your mind is yours and yours alone, a sacred space where you can nurture your dreams, tending to them like a gardener with a plot of delicate plants.

Recognize that your success isn't measured by scores on a test, but by the depth of your determination and the strength of your belief in yourself. You have to clear away the weeds of limiting beliefs to allow your dreams to take root and flourish.

Committing to a Skilled Trade

What has worked for me and countless others is embracing the transformational journey of pursuing a career in a skilled trade. My motivation for penning this book was to raise awareness that a rewarding life is very much attainable through a career in a skilled trade.

Picture yourself taking that decisive step, committing to an apprenticeship in a skilled trade. It's like planting a seed in fertile soil, nurturing it with time and effort, and watching it grow into a sturdy tree.

Redefining Success with Skilled Trades

I urge you to redefine success through the prism of skilled trades, embarking on a path less traveled, but one laden with opportunities and rewards that resonate with your true self.

You can become everything you ever imagined. Yes, you! The person reading these words right now. The realm of possibilities is as vast as the open sea waiting for you to sail through it, navigating toward your dream destination.

Benefits of Skilled Trades

Engage with this book as your guideline to success, as you unearth the treasures that a career in skilled trades can offer. Just like finding a hidden treasure chest, you will discover benefits such as a rewarding career and an income potential that is as expansive as the sky.

Imagine a world that aligns with you, that stands with you rather than against you. This can be your reality when you decide to embrace a skilled trade, a decision that promises not just a job but a fulfilling career.

The Path of a Skilled Tradesperson

In a world filled with uncertainties and bombarded with negativity from all corners, it's easy to lose sight of your dreams. But I assure you that, by choosing a skilled trade, you can reclaim the reins of your life, steering it in a direction where your dreams are not just figments of your imagination but attainable goals.

Embrace the fear of the unknown, see it as a challenge to overcome, a mountain to climb. Picture yourself reaching the peak, embracing the satisfaction of conquering your fears, and basking in the rewarding life that skilled trades promise.

The Unbeatable Advantage

This guarantee of an excellent salary does not come with a postsecondary education. A four-year degree in university leaves you in some cases with thousands of dollars in school loan debt, not to mention the four years spent without earning an income while you learn. This is time that could have been spent accumulating both experience and earnings.

Hands-on Experience

Also, upon completion, many find themselves with no on-site, hands-on work experience in the field they studied. Meanwhile, in the same amount of time that a university graduate finishes their degree, a tradesperson has usually completed their apprenticeship, boasting steady income coming in while they were mastering their trade.

Essentially, you would be four years ahead in earning an income, standing on a platform of practical knowledge and financial stability.

Instant Recognition

Instant gratification and credibility are solidified through the praise received from people around you when pursuing a skilled trade. I instantly became an expert in the field I chose. This journey made my family members proud — I had become the first electrical tradesperson in the family, an achievement that brought respect and recognition.

Building a Reputation

From day one, people were lining me up to do work for them, even when I was just starting. I took on the challenge and instantly began performing trade work for friends and family.

It wasn't just my experience; many others in different trade designations have had similar beginnings, finding themselves sought after almost as soon as they embarked on their chosen path.

More than Just a Job

Your experience might be as a hairdresser, where almost instantly after deciding to pursue this trade, you find yourself cutting friends' and family members' hair. It seems as though the people around you, perhaps even the universe, show just how proud they are of your decision.

It's a vivid demonstration of the respect and recognition that comes with being a skilled tradesperson.

A Lifelong Reward

So, why not decide to become one of the skilled people in this world, a master of your trade, a knowledgeable friend, and a go-to family member? People will turn to you throughout their lives, seeking advice and help from a seasoned tradesperson. The perception people have of you changes instantly — you morph into someone viewed as an expert in their field.

Harness the Power of Imagination

Can you imagine? I know you can... That's all you're required to do at this stage: envisage yourself thriving as a skilled tradesperson. Decide, commit, and embrace a life blessed with a rewarding career where giving and receiving become a harmonious cycle that spans a lifetime.

Choices Aplenty

With 144 skilled trades employment profiles to choose from in Ontario, the world is your oyster. Even at a young age, you can exercise your autonomy in making this life-altering decision. While advice from friends and family members can be valuable, this is a path that you can decide on all by yourself.

Uniting Passion and Profession

My experience has shown that friends and family members generally support a choice of a career in skilled trades. Skilled trades don't demand that you change who you are — they accept you, whole and complete, from any walk of life.

Decide

It all starts with that first, bold step. Decide today to pave a path filled with opportunities, learning, and growth. It's more than a job it's a rewarding career where your skills will always be in demand. It's a career where you can proudly say, "I am a master of my trade."

Summary

In this inaugural chapter titled "Decide," we embarked on the crucial first step of choosing to pursue an apprenticeship in the skilled trades. Grounded on the inspiring words of Steve Jobs, we explored the necessity of loving what you do to achieve great work. This step is far from trivial; it's about laying a robust foundation for a future filled with passion, and a sense of fulfillment in your chosen trade. It's a call to not settle for less but to find the path where your heart truly belongs. By embracing what you genuinely love, you give yourself the opportunity to immerse in work that doesn't feel like a chore but a fulfilling endeavor that nourishes your spirit daily.

Navigating through the initial stages, we emphasized the vitality of hands-on learning. This learning style not only offers a fresh start outside the traditional educational paradigms but also fosters a nurturing ground for acquiring real-life skills. It nurtures a proactive mindset where learning and doing go hand in hand, paving a road towards becoming proficient in your chosen trade. The chapter encourages you to envision a future where the apprenticeship shapes you into a professional equipped with skills derived not from textbooks but from tangible experiences, giving a rich depth to your understanding and approach toward your chosen field.

As we wrap up this chapter, it is hoped that a sense of clarity and determination has enveloped you, giving you a firm grounding as you stand at the threshold of a new beginning. This chapter was an encouragement, a nudge to take that brave step towards realizing your dream through a path less traversed, yet filled with rich learning experiences. Remember, the essence lies in the decision to pursue what you love, coupled with the perseverance to keep looking until you find it. Let this be your mantra as you forge ahead, sculpting a path characterized by passion, dedication, and an unwavering resolve to achieve greatness in your chosen field.

Chapter 2

Amperage of Your Apprenticeship

"The future belongs to those who prepare for it today."
— Malcolm X, Human Rights Activist

2

The Dawn of Your Apprenticeship

So, you've embarked on a remarkable journey into the dynamic world of skilled trades. This big step you've taken is like planting a seed, with dreams and aspirations packed in it, ready to grow and flourish as you nourish it with knowledge and hands-on experience. Let's set things in motion, making sure each step is carefully planned for a fruitful apprenticeship journey. Shall we dive in?

Early Bird Gets the Worm

You've likely heard this time-worn phrase throughout your life. Well, it's time to embody it. In the skilled trades, the early moments of the day are like the opening scenes of a film, setting the stage for the events to unfold. You are getting up before the sun, collecting yourself, breathing in the fresh morning air, and greeting the day with enthusiasm and readiness.

Consider this, like a baker rising in the early morning hours to knead the dough and prepare fresh bread, you are starting early, laying the foundations of a structure, one day at a time.

On-the-Go Meals

Imagine you're embarking on a grand adventure, like a hero in a story. Every hero needs sustenance to continue their journey. Packing a lunchbox with nourishing meals is akin to packing a treasure chest of energy that you can dip into throughout the day.

It's your personal stash of goodness, a constant in your day to fuel your body and mind, helping you to continue building, creating, and learning without losing steam.

Learning by Doing

Picture yourself building a giant Lego tower; each brick you add is a piece of knowledge, a skill acquired on the job. No more sitting idly in a classroom setting, feeling your enthusiasm wane with each passing minute. Now, you're right at the heart of the action, constructing your future with your own hands, one day at a time.

It's real, it's vibrant, and it's happening right before your eyes, as you piece together the puzzle of your trade, understanding and learning the how and why of each element that makes up your craft.

Incentives that Await

It's not unlike finding a golden ticket in your chocolate bar. As you forge your path in the skilled trades, there are provincial and federal government incentives waiting to be discovered. They're there to lend you a helping hand, to ease your financial burden, ensuring that your journey is not hampered by economic constraints.

It's a golden opportunity, a way to ease your pathway as you learn and grow in your chosen trade.

Tailored for You

Remember when you were a child, fascinated by the way things worked, always curious, always eager to explore? Your apprenticeship is a playground where your curiosity is not just welcomed but encouraged. It's time to embrace those qualities that make you, you. It's like swapping a pair of ill-fitting shoes for a pair that's just right, offering comfort, support, and a perfect fit. You're not just finding your place in the world of skilled trades; you're finding a place that feels like home, where learning feels natural, intuitive, and perfectly suited to you.

Recognizing Unique Learners

Remember the age-old saying, "Different strokes for different folks"? It rings true in this context. School isn't a one-size-fits-all experience, and recognizing that is like understanding that not every puzzle piece fits in every slot. There's an assortment of puzzle pieces, each unique and integral to the full picture, representing different types of learners. It's high time we encourage and foster the potential in students who resonate more with a hands-on approach, steering them toward a pathway of learning where they can truly shine.

Your Personal Pace

Your apprenticeship journey is akin to learning how to ride a bicycle. At first, you might wobble, perhaps move at a snail's pace as you find your balance. But with time, you find your unique pace, a comfortable speed at which you can cruise while enjoying the ride, absorbing the beauty around you. This personal pace, or "amperage," as we call it in the trades, sets the rhythm for your learning journey. It's your tune, one that suits your style, allowing you to dance through your apprenticeship with a rhythm that's uniquely yours.

The Art of Delayed Gratification

Embarking on an apprenticeship is much like nurturing a garden. It's about understanding that the beautiful bloom of a flower is the result of days, weeks, and even months of tender care and patience. As you sow the seeds of effort and water them with determination day by day, you foster a space for vibrant blossoms of success to thrive in the future. It's about stacking up small wins, like collecting precious stones on a hike, each one representing a milestone, a learned skill, or a job well done. These little trophies of daily triumphs create a path that leads you to the majestic view at the end of your trail—becoming a master in your skilled trade.

Navigating Highs and Lows

Just as a sailor navigates through calm seas and stormy weather, your apprenticeship journey will encompass periods of smooth sailing and times of challenges that test your mettle. It might sometimes feel like a mirage in a desert, the finish line appearing and then drifting further away. But remember, even when the journey seems like it's extending, with each step you are drawing closer to your goal.

It's a dance of patience and perseverance, a continuous waltz with highs that elevate you and lows that teach you, molding you into a resilient, skilled tradesperson.

Stay True to Your Path

Imagine you're building a tower with building blocks. Each layer represents a phase of your apprenticeship, a combination of work hours and theoretical learning at trade school. It's essential to maintain the integrity of your tower, to ensure each block is placed with consideration and determination, not sacrificing the quality of your structure for speed. Adhering to your personal schedule is like following a well laid out blueprint, it's a guiding light, a plan that ensures the magnificent tower you're building stands tall, strong, and splendid in the end.

Remember, the central character in this grand narrative is you, steering the ship steadfastly, with eyes fixed on the golden horizon of success that awaits.

Summary

In this chapter, you journeyed through the essential phase of organizing and navigating through your apprenticeship period. You dove into the world of preparing yourself to hit the ground running, right from setting your alarm for an early morning to ensuring a fulfilling meal to power through the day. This part of your journey is characterized by the symbiotic relationship between theory and practical skills garnered on the job site.

As we progressed, we delved into the nuances of personalized learning speeds, introducing the concept of the amperage of your apprenticeship. Through understanding the principle of delayed gratification, we ventured into the heart of apprenticeship life—a journey marred with both highs and lows. This chapter underscored the significance of perseverance, highlighting the vital role of both small and large wins accumulated over time. Through a realistic lens, we surveyed the general timeframe of an apprenticeship, cautioning against an unnecessary race against time, while encouraging patience and determination to endure and thrive during the apprenticeship period, respecting both its pace and process.

You stood on a note of self-empowerment, emphasizing your role as the central character in the apprenticeship narrative. You were encouraged to own your journey fiercely, asserting your needs and aligning your apprenticeship path with your personal schedule, emphasizing the non-negotiable nature of educational advancements.

Chapter 3

Calling on Anyone

*"What lies behind us and what lies before us are
tiny matters compared to what lies within us."*
— Ralph Waldo Emerson, American Essayist, Lecturer,
Philosopher, and Poet

3

A Calling for Everyone

L et's picture a garden, a vibrant and diverse one, with flowers of all kinds—tulips, roses, daisies, you name it. Each flower brings something special to the garden, making it richer and more colourful. The skilled trades industry is just like this garden, inviting and needing all sorts of talented individuals to flourish.

In this garden of opportunity, there's a spot for everyone — males, females, of all races and religions, every intellect level, different speech abilities, immigrants, and LGBTQ+ individuals. Yes, you heard it right, it's calling on anyone and everyone. It's a space where diversity isn't just welcomed; it's encouraged, nurtured, and celebrated.

The Constant Need for Skilled Trades

Imagine going to your favorite restaurant and finding out they've never run out of the secret ingredient that makes your favorite dish so delightful. Much like that secret ingredient, the demand for skilled tradespeople is ever-present, never dwindling, always essential.

In a rapidly changing job market, one thing remains unchangeable: the undying need for people proficient in skilled trades.

There's a noticeable gap, a spot waiting just for you, echoing a call for your unique set of skills and perspectives. Picture a jigsaw puzzle; it's incomplete without every single piece. You could be that missing piece, fitting perfectly, filling the gap, and completing the magnificent picture.

Not Just a Job, but a Fulfillment of Dreams

Think about when you were a child, drawing pictures with big, bold crayons, a canvas filled with dreams, colours, and no rules. A career in the skilled trades can be just like stepping back into that picture, where your character and creativity are not just allowed but encouraged.

A lot of us end up taking a job just for the sake of it, sometimes right after high school.

It's like choosing a bland dish over a flavorful one because it's right there. But why settle for less when you can have the best? Skilled trades offer a route where you don't just earn but learn, grow, and most importantly, enjoy what you do, satisfying that inner child with a canvas to paint your dreams on.

Remember the feeling when you got your first bicycle, and the world seemed just a little bit smaller, a bit more reachable? A career in the skilled trades can give you that feeling, but on a grand scale. It offers a pathway where you not only move forward but do so with a tool belt of skills that makes you a master of your destiny, painting your canvas with broad, confident strokes of a brush held firmly in your hand.

Come along as we delve deeper into this vibrant, colourful, and ever-welcoming world of skilled trades, a place where dreams aren't just dreamt but lived, every single day. It's a path where your unique hue adds to the masterpiece, a place where you're not just a worker, but an artist, a creator, crafting not just products, but a brighter future for yourself and the world. So, are you ready to find your colour in the skilled trades garden?

Hair Stylist — More than a Job, It's an Art

Picture yourself as a sculptor, but instead of clay, your canvas is hair, and your tools are scissors and brushes. Just like a painter with a blank canvas, the possibilities are endless, a realm of creativity just waiting for you to step in and start the newest trend, to craft something new, something uniquely yours.

As a hair stylist, you don't just cut hair; you shape dreams, carve style, and foster confidence in your clients. You get to sprinkle a bit of magic, turning a salon into a canvas of ever-changing trends and personal expressions. And who knows, with time and mastery, the salon could be your very own, a vibrant space echoing with the sounds of happy chatter and snipping scissors, a place reflecting your artistic vision.

Welder — Crafting Dreams with Steel

Imagine having the power to mold steel, a material as strong and unyielding as it sounds, into shapes and structures that were previously just visions in your mind. It's a bit like being a superhero, isn't it? You, with the might to bend steel, to craft monuments of art from a cold, lifeless material.

As you step into the world of welding, learning the craft piece by piece, understanding the different metals and their characteristics, it's almost like learning a new language, a language of creation through which you can speak your dreams into existence. And while five years of apprenticeship might seem like a mountain to climb, remember that even the longest journeys start with a single step, and every step you take is a step towards achieving your dream.

Growing Through Your Choices

Life is a series of choices, a continuous journey where every turn you take is guided by the decisions you make. A career in the skilled trades is not just a choice, it's an opportunity to grow, to bloom where you are planted, and to carve a path that resonates with your inner self.

Just as a tree grows and branches out, reaching new heights, you too can evolve and expand in your chosen field, nurturing your passions and, perhaps, discovering new ones along the way. The apprenticeship period is a golden time of realization, a time when dreams unfurl like buds blossoming into flowers, revealing opportunities and paths you never knew existed. It's a time of nurturing your mindset, allowing it to grow and expand, much like a gardener tending to a prized plant, nourishing it to bloom in full splendor.

Join us as we continue this journey, a path where your dreams are not just dreams, but seeds of reality, ready to grow into a garden of opportunities, a life rich with satisfaction, and a future crafted by your hands, guided by your passions, and fueled by your dedication. Ready to take the first step? Let's forge your path together in the fulfilling world of skilled trades.

An Open Door to All

Imagine a realm where doors swing open wide for every person, irrespective of their background, gender, or sexual orientation. This is the vibrant and inclusive world of skilled trades, a place where the only prerequisite is the willingness to dream, learn, and put in the dedicated hours to hone a craft.

Just as a rainbow encompasses an array of colours, the skilled trades welcome a spectrum of individuals—be it a male hairstylist painting the town with the latest trends, a female crane operator orchestrating heavy machinery with finesse, or a female baker crafting cakes that tell a thousand stories. Picture the beauty of diversity reflected in a prismatic spray of sparks flying from a welder's torch; it's a testament to the inclusive spirit of the trades.

Breaking Stereotypes and Building Dreams

Think about it, when was the last time you crossed paths with a gay plumber or a queer tool and die maker? In the rich tapestry of the skilled trades, everyone has a place, a role, and an opportunity to shatter stereotypes, proving that nothing is out of reach, and no dream is too grand.

It's a bit like an artist breaking away from traditional canvases to create masterpieces on unexpected mediums, constantly evolving, constantly surprising. Here, the word 'impossible' is replaced with 'I'm possible,' and every day is a fresh canvas waiting for you to paint it with your unique shade of brilliance, fostering a place where character, nobility, and credibility are not just words but lived experiences.

Identifying Your Path

You see, the world of skilled trades is like a vast garden, brimming with opportunities, just waiting for you to find your perfect patch under the sun. It beckons you to follow your passions and play to your strengths, fostering a nurturing ground for your interests to flourish.

Picture yourself walking down a path lined with various trades, each calling out to different facets of your personality, urging you to explore and discover that one special niche that resonates with your inner self. It's a journey of self-discovery, where following your heart is not just encouraged but is the key to finding your place in this ever-evolving landscape of opportunities.

Join us as we tread this path of inclusivity and diversity, a journey towards a future carved out of determination, a passion nurtured through perseverance, and dreams brought to life through skilled hands and nurturing hearts. Let's champion the spirit of skilled trades, where every individual is a vital thread in this rich and vibrant tapestry, crafting a future brimming with possibilities and a workforce as diverse as a rainbow, ready to dazzle with every hue of skill and talent. Are you ready to find your colour in the rainbow of skilled trades? Let's step forward together.

Summary

In the vast and colourful realm of skilled trades, every individual finds a welcoming embrace, a place that celebrates diversity in all its glorious shades and nuances. This chapter journeyed through the expansive landscape of opportunities in skilled trades, illustrating that it is a field open to all, regardless of gender, sexuality, or background. Like a garden waiting to be explored, the skilled trades offer a nurturing ground where every dream has the space to take root and flourish. It's a place where the canvas of life waits, ready for you to paint it with strokes of your individuality, bringing to life dreams that are as diverse as they are beautiful.

As we navigated the world of skilled trades, we saw how it champions the breaking of stereotypes, encouraging each person to carve out a niche that resonates with their true self. It's a domain where character, nobility, and credibility are not just words but a living testament to the spirit of perseverance and the joy of crafting with one's own hands. Like a master artist who continually seeks out new mediums to express themselves, this field encourages innovation and the breaking of norms, welcoming a future where 'impossible' is replaced with 'I'm possible.'

We wrapped up our exploration underscoring the pivotal role of self-discovery in this journey through skilled trades. It's a path of following your heart, of tuning into your natural abilities and interests to forge a career that's not just rewarding but also deeply fulfilling. Picture yourself in a garden of possibilities, each trade a different path lined with opportunities waiting to be discovered. It's an invitation to dream, to grow, and to find that one special niche where you can shine the brightest. As we stand at the brink of this exciting journey, the skilled trades beckon with a rainbow of opportunities, encouraging you to find your unique colour in this vibrant tapestry. It's a call to step forward into a world brimming with potential, where every day is a fresh canvas waiting for you to add your hue of brilliance. Let's step forward together, into a future crafted with skilled hands and nurturing hearts, into a world as diverse and dazzling as a rainbow.

Chapter 4

Women in Trades

"Do not wait for leaders; do it alone, person to person."
— Mother Teresa, Roman Catholic Nun, Missionary & Nobel
Peace Prize Winner

4

A New Dawn for Women in Skilled Trades

Just as a majestic tree doesn't conform to the space it's allotted, always seeking to grow higher and broader, you too have the chance to stretch beyond traditionally defined boundaries, reaching for skies previously thought unreachable. Picture yourself standing in a vast field of opportunities, a place where you are not defined by pre-existing norms but by your passion and dedication. In this new era, the skilled trades have emerged as a vibrant and inclusive platform, creating a rich tapestry where every thread, regardless of its origin, contributes to a larger, more beautiful picture.

As we steer away from outdated norms, we find ourselves at a pivotal moment in history where an equal representation of genders in the trades is not just a possibility, but a blossoming reality.

Discover the Boundless Opportunities

Imagine opening a treasure chest of 144 different skilled trades, each one a sparkling gem offering a world of possibilities. As you delve deeper, you come to realize that the skilled trades landscape is a rich, vibrant ecosystem where creativity meets opportunity, offering a nurturing ground for growth and expression that rivals any office job. Just like choosing the ripest fruit from a tree, you have the liberty to choose a path that suits you, be it carving elegant furniture, fashioning stunning pieces of clothing, or sculpting steel into marvelous art.

The trades offer a canvas where your creativity knows no bounds, a place where daily accomplishments aren't just acknowledged but celebrated. Picture yourself standing tall, a beacon of creativity and determination, embodying the spirit of a modern tradeswoman, a leader paving the way for others to follow.

Redefining Strength and Creativity

Venturing into the skilled trades as a woman is akin to setting forth on a grand adventure, where every day presents a new challenge to overcome, a new height to scale. Yes, the path might be strewn with hurdles, the initial stages demanding both mental and physical stamina, but remember, just as a diamond is formed under pressure, so will your skills be honed through perseverance.

Forget the outdated notions of what it means to work in trades—envision instead a workplace where your unique perspective as a woman is not only welcomed but desired, where your creativity finds a natural home, blooming in the most unexpected places. It's a world where strength isn't defined by physical might alone, but by resilience, ingenuity, and the courage to carve out your own path, shining brightly, a beacon of change in a transforming landscape.

Visualize the Infinite Pathways

As you stand on the brink of this exciting journey, remember that skilled trades are not a destination but a journey filled with rich experiences and learning curves, a pathway laden with opportunities waiting to be seized. Whether it's uniting with fellow craftspeople in a union, spearheading your entrepreneurial venture, or immersing yourself in the world of creative design, the trades offer a universe of opportunities, ripe for exploration.

Just like a river constantly forging new paths, creating rivulets and streams, your journey in the skilled trades will be one of continuous growth, evolving with every step you take. It's a call to embrace a world rich with potential, where dreams take flight, nurtured by skilled hands and innovative minds, ready to shape the future with a spirit unbounded and a vision uncontained. Let's champion this changing landscape, stepping boldly into a future where the sky is not the limit but just the beginning.

Crafting Your Unique Trade Journey

Picture a canvas, initially blank but pulsating with potential. This is the fertile ground that skilled trades offer you, a space where your visions take shape, fueled by diligence, expertise, and creativity. Much like a seasoned gardener, you have the liberty to cultivate a landscape of creativity, merging art with trade to create a garden of wonders where dreams blossom into reality. Inspirational women in the sector stand as towering trees, testimony to the fact that with a strong foundation in skilled trades, your branches can stretch far and wide, reaching into spheres you had only dared to dream of.

As you venture into research, uncovering stories of triumphant tradeswomen, you'll find that it echoes the thrilling tales of adventurers discovering new lands, mapping out paths previously untraveled, showing you the grand vistas that await. Just as every great artist starts with learning the basics, mastering the brush strokes before painting their masterpiece, in the skilled trades too, you start with mastering your craft, a journey where perseverance transforms insecurities into mastery, and doubts into self-assurance.

The Symphony of Art and Skilled Trades

Imagine stepping into a grand gallery where each piece of art narrates a tale of passion, determination, and skill. This gallery is the vibrant world of skilled trades, where each day is a new canvas for you to paint your story. It is a realm where art and skilled trade dance in harmony, creating a symphony of work-life satisfaction that reverberates through every aspect of your life. It is the celebration of self-sufficiency, a tribute to the harmonious merger of mind and hand, and the triumph of seeing dreams crystallize into tangible creations, much like a sculptor revealing the statue hidden within the stone.

By shedding the cocoon of traditional mindsets, you unveil a butterfly of opportunities, soaring high, creating patterns of success, vibrant with colours of satisfaction and self-expression.

Embrace this evolving artistry, for in the theater of skilled trades, you are both the playwright and the star, scripting a saga of unbounded creativity and unprecedented achievements.

Fostering Diversity and Breaking Stereotypes

Step into the empowering arena of skilled trades where diversity is not just encouraged but celebrated. Envision bustling job sites where women excel as carpenters, welders, and plumbers, weaving a rich tapestry of skills, an evolving picture that shatters outdated norms with each confident stroke. It's a dynamic mosaic that is continuously being crafted with equal measures of strength, courage, and artistry, portraying a vivid story of modern tradeswomen triumphantly steering their destinies.

As you stand in this vivid landscape, realize that this is not just a projection of a hopeful future, but a reality being sculpted right now. Companies championing all-female workforces stand as beacon towers, illuminating the path for many more to follow, echoing the vibrant chorus of diversity and equality, a testament to a society that has matured, embracing the beautiful diversity that is a true representation of its strength.

Yes, the path might have its share of twists and turns, but remember, just like the most exhilarating stories are filled with adventures and unexpected twists, your journey in skilled trades promises to be a riveting tale of growth, achievements, and breaking free from the shackles of stereotypes to craft a future where you are the master of your destiny. Let your story be one of courage, creativity, and unyielding spirit, a vivid tapestry of a tradeswoman's journey, rich with hues of passion, determination, and fulfillment.

Paving the Way for the Future Tradeswoman

Imagine a world where comfort meets professionalism. A space where every woman feels at ease having another skilled woman manage repairs in her residence, a reflection of empathy and understanding forged from shared experiences. It's a growing trend where contracting companies not only advocate but encourage and nurture women to step into roles traditionally held by men, facilitating a journey where dreams and reality walk hand in hand.

In this evolving landscape, women are not just employees but also thriving entrepreneurs who helm contracting companies, steering them to success with determination and skill. It dismantles the myth that physical work is synonymous with brute strength, highlighting that the true requisites are dexterity, stamina, and excellent hand-eye coordination–attributes not limited by gender but shared equally among men and women.

Sculpting New Norms

Visualize a workplace where the norm is equality, where women bring a unique perspective, shaping a rich and diverse tapestry with their individuality and creativity. It is a place where voices are valued, where innovative ideas are encouraged, fostering a collaborative environment that drives projects forward with optimal decisions.

Today, the spotlight is rightly being cast on the abundant opportunities awaiting women in the skilled trades. Organizations like Women in Skilled Trades and the Canadian Women's Foundation stand as guardians, equipped with the tools and training needed to usher women into the realm of construction, fostering skills and nurturing talents for a fulfilling career.

A Flourishing Future with Skilled Trades

As you stand on the threshold of opportunities, know that the industry and even the Canadian government are rallying to elevate gender diversity in skilled trades, a move steered towards creating a balanced, integrated workplace that echoes profitability and progress. With initiatives like the Canadian Apprenticeship Service & Aboriginal Apprenticeship Board, a new horizon opens up for women in Red Seal trades, encouraging broader industry participation, and fostering a realm where dreams are not just envisioned but achieved.

Envision a career path where you, as a woman, can merge your entire skill set, a path where learning is accompanied by earning, a journey where perseverance meets opportunity. Whether it is carving a lifelong career or using it as a stepping stone to realize your true potential, skilled trades open the door to a world of possibilities, where your dreams are validated, nurtured, and brought to fruition.

It is a call to every woman with a spirit of leadership, a zest for learning, and a heart brimming with aspirations to seize the opportunities that lie in the skilled trades. It is an invitation to explore, learn, and grow in a field replete with opportunities, where your dreams find a solid ground to take root and flourish into a vibrant reality.

As you step forward, remember that this path, rich with opportunities, is not just a career but a testament to your strength, adaptability, and determination to succeed. Forge ahead with unwavering belief in yourself, for in the skilled trades, your dreams are not just valid but await to be sculpted into magnificent realities through your hard work and dedication.

It's a realm where the skilled tradeswoman doesn't just build structures, but constructs her destiny, one determined step at a time. So venture forward, for a fulfilling, empowered future awaits to be crafted by your skilled hands and visionary mind.

Summary

In this chapter, we delved deep into the dynamic landscape of skilled trades, focusing particularly on the evolving role and opportunities for women in this sector. We demystified outdated notions surrounding physical capabilities and gender, emphasizing that dexterity, stamina, and hand-eye coordination—attributes that both men and women equally possess — are the primary requirements in skilled trades. Highlighting the shift from tradition, we portrayed a reality where women are not just employees but successful entrepreneurs, running contracting companies with skill and determination. The narrative implores women to envision themselves in various roles across the 144 skilled trades available, emphasizing that a career in this sector promises not just financial stability but a platform to express one's creativity and ingenuity.

Building on the idea of change, we took readers on a journey showcasing the increasingly inclusive environment of skilled trades. Here, the focus is on the unique perspectives women bring to the table, creating a rich tapestry of ideas and fostering collaboration that drives optimal decision-making in projects. Moreover, we highlighted the supportive network ready to assist women in embarking on careers in this field, with organizations like Women in Skilled Trades and the Canadian Women's Foundation providing tools and training to nurture talent. This section sheds light on how colleges and institutions are creating low-cost apprenticeship programs specifically geared toward women, encouraging them to take the helm in an industry ready to embrace diversity.

As we rounded off the chapter, the spotlight was on the proactive role of the Canadian government in promoting gender diversity through initiatives such as the Canadian Apprenticeship Service. This not only showcases a government committed to fostering diversity but also echoes a larger shift in industry perspectives, with companies increasingly recognizing the value of a diverse workforce. We encouraged women to seize the plethora of opportunities lying in the skilled trades, urging them to forge paths where they are not just working but crafting legacies through careers that reflect their passion and skills. The closing note is a call to action, a plea for women to embrace the skilled trades, nurturing their talents, and carving out successful careers, while shaping a future where gender diversity is not just a goal but a norm.

Chapter 5

In Canada, All Dreams Come True

"The only limit to our realization
of tomorrow is our doubts of today."
— Franklin D. Roosevelt, 32nd President of the United States

5

Bridging the Skills Gap with Immigrant Expertise

We begin this chapter with a glaring fact–Canada is experiencing a shortage of over a million trade workers. This void presents a grand landscape of opportunities as about 40% of all job openings in the foreseeable future will be in the skilled trades. This is not just a matter of numbers; it's an urgent call to action to bridge the 'skills gap' with innovative and inclusive solutions.

Trade Careers: A Beacon of Hope for New Canadians

The skilled trades sector is not just about bolstering the economy, it's about enriching the lives of the individuals who are part of it, particularly those who are embarking on a fresh start in Canada.

As a new or prospective resident of Canada, envision forging a fulfilling and dynamic career in the skilled trades, a sector teeming with prospects for both genders and people from all walks of life. Picture yourself leveraging a trade certificate as a potent tool, a springboard to a future brimming with opportunities and financial stability.

Building Dreams with Skilled Hands

What does it take to carve out such a success story in Canada's skilled trade sector? The answer lies in marrying your mind and hand skills to take advantage of learning opportunities in project-based careers, which potentially offer annual salaries around the region of 80,000 dollars.

The path to this vibrant life in Canada is paved with determination, a clear focus on acquiring a skilled trade, and the courage to overcome hurdles such as foreign educational credential setbacks and language barriers, much like the many immigrants who have successfully done so before. The rich tapestry of Canada's workforce has been woven with threads of perseverance and hard work of countless immigrants, and this chapter invites you to become a part of this inspiring narrative.

A Rewarding Path with Tangible Benefits

Imagine landing a job where stability isn't just a catchphrase but a vivid reality reflected in the substantial benefits like a sound pension plan, guaranteed holidays, and of course, job security—much like the comfort and predictability that comes with a home equipped with all necessary amenities. This path isn't just about earning a livelihood, it's akin to being a vital cog in a larger mechanism, contributing significantly to Canada and its ever-evolving landscape.

As a new Canadian, you're not just filling a role, you are stepping into a sphere where your work is akin to that of an artist crafting masterpieces, actively contributing to reducing the labor shortage through a high-skill, high-wage career in construction or trades.

Safety and Respect: The Canadian Workplace Culture

Entering the Canadian workforce is like stepping into a place where your safety and wellbeing are prioritized, a refreshing change especially for those coming from environments with a more lax approach to safety measures. Imagine being in a place where skilled tradespeople are held in high esteem, a reverence somewhat resembling the respect accorded to a seasoned craftsman who is well-versed in creating remarkable pieces from raw materials. In this nurturing environment, every skilled immigrant is a valuable asset, much like a rare jewel that adds value and sparkle to the Canadian economic tapestry.

This sense of respect and appreciation is a common thread in the Canadian workspace, painting a picture of dignity and value that is sometimes reminiscent of a well-loved community elder, who garners respect through wisdom and experience.

Turning Dreams into Reality with the Federal Skilled Trades Program

If this narrative resonates with you or someone you know residing in a foreign country, here is a golden pathway to transform dreams into reality—the Federal Skilled Trades

Program. This initiative is somewhat like a dedicated guidance counselor in a school, helping students find their true calling based on their innate strengths and skills. Administered by Immigration, Refugees, and Citizenship Canada (IRCC), it takes on the vital role of meticulously going through your credentials, just as a librarian might sort through books to find the perfect title for a reader, ensuring you are placed appropriately in a role where you can flourish.

The potential paths are vast and varied, not dissimilar to the expansive aisles in a supermarket, each offering a different flavor of opportunities; they range from major groupings such as electrical and construction trades to minor groups like culinary roles including chefs and bakers.

Navigating the Immigration Process

Stepping into Canada through the Federal Skilled Trades Program is like acquiring a golden ticket to a land of opportunities. It stipulates having a confirmed job waiting for you, akin to having a well-paved road directing you to your destination. This pathway allows you to achieve a certificate of qualification in your chosen skilled trade, setting a firm foundation, much like the bedrock that holds up a sturdy building.

Moreover, the express entry feature functions somewhat like a rewards program, where your educational endeavors can earn you valuable points, ensuring your academic credentials find their worthy equivalent in the Canadian educational landscape.

Express Entry: A Gateway to Opportunities

The express entry system works tirelessly, somewhat reminiscent of a meticulous gardener nurturing plants to bloom, aiding skilled workers in their journey to becoming permanent residents in Canada. It undertakes the serious responsibility of verifying your educational credentials, ensuring it stands tall, comparable to a well-regarded Canadian secondary or postsecondary credential — a process akin to a quality check ensuring you receive a product that meets the highest standards.

It's not just a system; it's a bridge connecting potential high-skilled foreign workers to a life woven with opportunities and promise in Canada.

Building a Career with Rich Potential

Canada's work landscape, with its rich tapestry of creative, motivated, and diverse workforce, stands as a testament to its strength and unique identity—it's like a vibrant mosaic where each piece contributes to creating a beautiful, unified image. Here, diversity isn't just encouraged; it's celebrated, fostering a work environment where equal opportunities reign supreme, safeguarding individuals from any form of discrimination.

As a newcomer, preparing yourself is akin to sharpening your tools before embarking on a significant project. Taking up courses in English or French, along with certifications in First Aid, CPR, and WHMIS, not only enhances your skill set but also showcases you as a candidate with maximum potential, ready to carve out a niche in the skilled trades sector in Canada.

Summary

You learned that Canada needs many more people to work in skilled trades, and this is a great chance for new Canadians, including women and people moving to Canada from other countries, to find good jobs. The chapter tells us that learning a trade can be a great start in Canada, helping people earn a good living and take care of their families. It talks about how, even though moving to a new place can be hard, many people have done it successfully before, using their skills and determination to build a good life in Canada.

The second part of the chapter discusses how new Canadians can find good jobs that not only pay well but also come with benefits like holidays and job security. It says that working in a trade can be a way to do something important for Canada while also taking care of one's own family. The chapter introduces the Federal Skilled Trades Program which helps people find the right trade for them from a big list of job options, and talks about the kind of jobs one can find in this, like being a chef or working in construction.

Also, this chapter talks about the steps a person needs to take to move to Canada and start working in a trade. It mentions the Express Entry system that helps in checking if a person's education from another country matches with the Canadian education standards. The chapter encourages new people coming to Canada to learn English or French, and take other courses to help them do well in their jobs here, kind of like adding extra toppings on a pizza to make it even better. It ends with a message of hope, saying that with the right skills and hard work, anyone can find success in Canada.

Chapter 6

Fear of Power

"Power is not given to you. You have to take it."
— Beyoncé Knowles-Carter, American Singer,
Songwriter, and Actress

6

Recapping the Journey and Taking the First Bold Step

In previous chapters, we journeyed through the open arms of the skilled trades world, exploring its inclusivity and the windows it opens for people from diverse backgrounds including the LGBTQ+ community, women, aboriginals, and immigrants. Now, let's circle back to the pivotal moment of making a choice, the seed from which the tree of a fulfilling career grows.

Deciding to venture down this road isn't a walk in the park; it is more akin to standing at a crossroad where each path leads to a different adventure. It means embracing a commitment that spans several years, painting a canvas that stretches wide and far, where each stroke represents the dedication and hard work you put in.

A Dive into the Unknown

I recall the hesitations clouding my mind, much like a ship on the verge of venturing into uncharted waters when the opportunity to apprentice as an electrician was laid out in front of me. Even with a mantle adorned with recognition like "Employee of the Year" at a previous workplace, the journey seemed like stepping into a room blindfolded, every step into the unknown echoed with questions and fears.

But here's where I urge you to remember the brave choice of saying "yes," akin to opening a book to immerse yourself into a world filled with opportunities, a world sculpted from hard work and sheer determination.

Reflections on an Unplanned Path

It wasn't a straight highway drive for me; rather, my path twisted and turned, venturing into the realms of skilled trades a good few years post high school. It was not a childhood dream but a passion discovered in the backyard of the early twenties, showcasing that the doors to skilled trades stand wide open at various stages of life, inviting in anyone with a heart brimming with determination and a spirit ready to dive in. It's akin to finding a hidden trail in a familiar forest, one that promises new adventures and vistas of opportunities that I hadn't considered before.

It's never too late to change the course and sail towards the islands of skilled trades, to carve out a niche that resonates with one's intrinsic self, evolving with each step forward in this chosen pathway. The key lesson here is the empowerment embedded in decision-making, how it unfurls a roadmap dotted with milestones that mark personal growth and self-fulfillment.

It is about writing a story with a pen held firmly, inscribing experiences with conviction and a heart full of hope for what lays on the next page. It speaks to the vibrant variety in the landscape of skilled trades, a landscape where dreams find ground and grow into strong, towering trees under the nurturing sun of hard work and perseverance.

A Collision with Fear and Wonder

When I first brushed up against the world of electricity, it felt like standing before a large, magnificent but slightly scary painting — a world full of wonder yet shrouded in mystery, a topic that seemed to resonate with intelligence and demanded respect. You might feel the same, it could be akin to staring at a giant jigsaw puzzle with a thousand pieces, where every piece is vital, and there's an initial fear of not knowing where to start.

To me, back then, electricity bore an intimidating face, something like a giant roller coaster ride that promises thrills but also invokes a healthy dose of fear. The notion that it was a field reserved for the super smart, the math geniuses, hung over me like a cloud, shadowing my confidence.

The Weekend of Reflection

The offer to apprentice came as an unexpected gift, much like finding a rare gem in a pile of stones. It was handed to me by a gentleman who saw potential in me, a potential that I hadn't yet realized.

His encouragement to mull it over felt like being handed a golden ticket but being too nervous to use it right away. It was a weekend of wrestling with inner demons of doubt, akin to pacing in a room with many doors, each leading to a different future, and feeling the pressure of choosing the right one. My mind swirled in a whirlpool of questions, much like a leaf caught in a brisk wind, unsure where it would land.

The complexity echoed the feelings you might have when presented with a path that promises growth but also demands stepping out of comfort zones, much like a bird contemplating its first flight from the nest.

The Transformation Begins

Turning to my father felt like reaching for a trusted guidebook, a source of wisdom grounded in experience, and his words were simple yet profound. "You're good with your hands." He presented me with a mirror, urging me to look beyond perceived limitations, much like a wise teacher encouraging a hesitant student to trust in their abilities.

It's as if he handed me a pair of glasses, helping me to see the possibilities clearly, showing that the world of electricity wasn't just for mathematicians but for anyone with the curiosity to explore and the will to learn. It became clear that skill wasn't just about having a brain filled with knowledge but also having hands skilled in craft and a heart ready to embrace challenges.

By Monday, with a brave spirit, much like a soldier ready for battle, I said *'yes'* to the apprenticeship, ready to carve a path in the electrifying world of electrical trades.

Starting that journey felt like stepping into a new world with eyes wide open, ready to absorb, learn, and grow, much like a sapling reaching towards the sun, eager to grow tall and strong. I hope as you read this, you realize that saying 'yes' can be the starting point of a transformative journey, one that takes you from a place of self-doubt to a space brimming with opportunities, painting your canvas of life with rich experiences and learning.

This path, albeit filled with hard work and challenges, promises to shape you into someone new, ready to face life with a newfound skill and confidence, much like a caterpillar evolving into a butterfly, ready to spread its wings and fly. Remember, the power to take this monumental step lies within you; it's all about taking that first determined step, akin to the brave first stroke on a blank canvas, initiating a masterpiece in the making.

Summary

I revisited the earlier discussions of the skilled trades world, recognizing the significant choice to pursue a career within it—a decision that is both intimidating and exhilarating. The path isn't easy, it's a commitment that demands dedication and hard work, much like an artist contributing to a vast canvas. I shared my apprehensions about starting an apprenticeship in electricity, likening it to stepping blindfolded into an unknown room. Despite previous successes and accolades, the uncertainty of this new endeavor is palpable, filled with questions and fears. Yet, I also recounted the empowerment of embracing this opportunity, urging myself and others to say "yes" to the journey ahead, filled with hard work and determination.

Reflecting on my unexpected journey into skilled trades, I noted that it wasn't a childhood ambition but a passion discovered in my early twenties. The entry into this field is not time-bound, it's open to anyone at any stage of life who possesses the determination to learn and the readiness to dive in. I liken my experience to discovering a hidden path in a well-known forest, filled with new adventures and unforeseen opportunities. This chapter serves as a reminder of the power of decision-making, how it creates a personal roadmap marked by milestones of growth and self-fulfillment.

Finally, I described the initial collision with the world of electricity—awe-inspiring but also intimidating. The weekend that followed the offer to apprentice was fraught with self-doubt and a whirlwind of questions, much like a leaf caught in a brisk wind. It was a moment of deep contemplation, akin to standing at the threshold of numerous paths, each leading to a different destiny. Seeking guidance, I turned to my father, whose advice was a beacon, leading me to see beyond my limitations. By Monday, with renewed bravery, I accepted the apprenticeship, ready to embark on a transformative journey into the world of electrical trades. This decision marked the beginning of a new chapter in my life, one that promises not just personal development but also the shaping of a new identity, as I learn to navigate life with a new set of skills and confidence.

Chapter 7

Journeyperson / Master Electrician Years

"To be a master at any skill, it takes the total effort of
your heart, mind, and soul working together in tandem."
— Maurice Young, American Rapper, Songwriter, and Actor

7

Journeyperson Wisdom from Don McIsaac

Firstly, imagine this, you've got your journeyperson license tucked safely in your pocket, a symbol of all your hard work, the tough days, and the knowledge you've gathered during your apprenticeship. It feels like holding a golden ticket, doesn't it? But in the insightful words of the wise Don McIsaac, a decade in your trade is what truly rounds you, and molds you into a reliable, resourceful journeyperson.

Ten years of dedication, going to different sites, and facing various challenges, it is like gradually adding colours to your painter's palette until you have a full array to create any picture imaginable.

The Treasure of Experience at Holley Electric

Recall my time spent nurturing my skills at Holley Electric, where my tool belt is filled not just with tools, but with golden nuggets of experience in service and installation. There's a certain beauty in not being limited to either commercial or residential environments, isn't there? It's like being a chef who can cook both hearty home meals and fancy restaurant dishes, being able to adapt and serve in any setting.

Each service call I responded to was a mystery, a puzzle to solve. Sometimes you had the key to solve it, other times you created the key on the spot with a cocktail of confidence, luck, and knowledge. It was learning to dance gracefully even when you didn't know all the steps, giving your audience a performance they would applaud, despite the turmoil swirling in your head.

The Continuous Journey of Learning

But being a journeyperson isn't just about fixing things. It's steering the ship through large jobs, from the embryonic stage of drafting scopes of work to the triumphant moment of passing the final inspection. It's a role that demands a beautiful symphony of planning, supervising, and evolving continuously, a bit like a gardener nurturing plants from seeds to full bloom, overseeing every little detail, down to the tiniest nuts and bolts.

And just like a tree growing stronger and branching out, your skill set too, branches out into areas unexplored. You find yourself stepping into the shoes of a project manager, drawing upon the wealth of knowledge and expertise you gathered as a journeyperson. Visualizing a project becomes like storytelling, where you sketch the beginning, visualize the plot, and foresee a successful ending, including the smallest details in your narrative, enhancing your proficiency in time and material tasks or pricing jobs.

As you turn the pages of your career, remember that learning is a road that goes ever on and on, a path filled with opportunities to learn, to grow, and to become not just a master of your craft, but a master of adaptability, ready to face any challenge that comes your way with a spirit of curiosity and determination.

It is a journey where every day is a fresh canvas, waiting for you to paint it with the colours of your experience and knowledge. So, gear up for this continuous voyage of evolution, where every day is a step towards becoming a timeless masterpiece in your trade.

Mastering the Art of Detail

Imagine being an artist, carefully selecting and arranging colours on your palette before starting a masterpiece. Similarly, being trusted with time and material jobs entails meticulous preparation, with you precisely curating a detailed material list for your boss, a skill that paints you as a diligent and trustworthy worker in the eyes of your employer. It's like being the meticulous planner in a group trip, ensuring every detail is noted, so the journey goes off without a hitch.

This attention to the finer details, to inches and millimeters, becomes a canvas of potential success, leading to installations that fit seamlessly, avoiding the chaotic scramble that often accompanies ill-prepared projects.

Sketching the Blueprint of Success

Now, consider the journey of a craftsman, who uses a sketchbook as a trusted companion, a space to conceptualize, measure, and create a blueprint, taking it from the site to the office, almost like a chef taking notes of a secret recipe to recreate in their kitchen. It is through these sketches that the right materials are ordered and the necessary components fabricated.

Think of it as preparing a complex dish, where the proper sequence of adding ingredients matters, ensuring a harmonious blend of flavors, and setting a stage for a seamless flow in the installation process.

Becoming a Beacon of Learning

As you sharpen your skills in drawing and planning, envision a tree growing tall, branching out, ready to offer shade and fruits to others. In a similar vein, you turn into a mentor, a repository of knowledge ready to nurture the saplings, the apprentices under your wings, sharing the wisdom accumulated over years, becoming not just a supervisor, but potentially a master and even a company owner.

This journey of growth and learning mirrors a thriving ecosystem where everyone learns and grows together, fostering a culture of collective growth and learning.

Your career as a journeyperson becomes a vibrant, ever-evolving painting, where with every stroke of experience, you add depth and richness to your professional canvas, creating a better version of yourself. The trade becomes more than just a job, it's a rich narrative of continuous learning, a stepping stone to a landscape brimming with opportunities, where the hunger for knowledge doesn't just enhance your skills but becomes a beacon, lighting the path for others to follow, creating a vibrant, learning community that constantly evolves, adapts, and flourishes.

Remember, the journeyperson's role is vital, a mentor guiding the future generation, crafting not just projects but shaping adept hands and thoughtful minds, laying down the bricks for a future filled with skilled and wise individuals.

The Journey from Student to Teacher

In the realm of skilled trade, imagine your journey as evolving from a humble student to a wise teacher, much like a curious child growing to become a nurturing parent, guiding the next generation with wisdom distilled from personal experiences.

As you embrace the role of a mentor, you craft lessons with your unique touch, sifting through your knowledge and retaining only the golden nuggets, the tactics that truly made a difference in your journey. Picture yourself as a gardener, carefully selecting the best seeds—the finest approaches and strategies that worked for you—to plant in the fertile mind of your apprentice.

Cultivating Patience and Positivity

In this nurturing ground, it's essential to foster a garden of patience and positivity. Encourage your apprentice to learn from mistakes, likening it to a chef perfecting a recipe through trial and error, reassuring them that materials like pipes are abundant and there to be experimented with, and mistakes are just stepping stones in the path to mastery.

A negative approach would be like trying to grow a plant by stifling it, but a positive, patient mentorship is the sunshine that allows your apprentice to flourish, encouraging them to respect others and to perceive their work as a significant piece in a vast puzzle of interrelated crafts.

Building Bridges Between Trades

Delve deeper into the puzzle analogy, explaining how each trade forms a unique piece that comes together harmoniously to create a beautiful picture, a finished project.

Showcase the synergy between trades with everyday examples, like the installation of an electric hot water tank, where an electrician and a plumber work hand in hand, each playing their role much like a duet creating a beautiful piece of music with their respective instruments. This part of the learning is akin to teaching a child to play well with others, developing a harmony that respects the strengths of everyone involved.

Mastering Customer Service

As you approach the end of this teaching journey, emphasize the golden rule of customer service, painting it as the cherry on top of a job well done. Picture yourself as a host at a party, where communication and making your guests—in this case, customers—feel valued and respected, are just as important as the main event.

Remind them that beyond being excellent at their job, it's vital to wear a smile, to be the kind tradesperson who leaves a warm memory in the client's mind, assuring no callbacks and fostering a lasting relationship. It's about crafting a service with both skill and heart, building a reputation that stands tall like a lighthouse, and guiding more opportunities your way because of the radiant energy of positivity and respect you emanate in your trade. Encourage them to create a legacy of not just a tradesperson, but a tradesperson who touches hearts with service that goes beyond mere technical excellence.

Becoming a Guiding Force

You might find yourself sent into a myriad of situations as a journeyperson. You could be walking into a project that hasn't been going as planned, and yet, everyone looks at you to steady the ship. It's like being the person who always has a spare tire, someone everyone relies on in sticky situations.

Your capability to handle these tough spots not only soothes concerned customers but also makes you a golden asset in your boss's eyes. Imagine yourself as a gardener who knows just how to prune a tree to coax the best blossoms out of it.

The Magic of Great Customer Service

As you groom yourself in this role, you'll find that interviewers in today's world are keen on understanding how you maneuver through challenging situations. It's like they are more interested in seeing the seasoned sailor in you than the one who just knows how to steer in calm waters.

You are no longer just a candidate with a resumé; you are a story of resilience, adaptability, and resourcefulness. Think of it as having a superpower, the "how can I help you" approach, which unfolds a myriad of opportunities and rewards in front of you. It's the comforting hug that everyone appreciates, setting you a class apart from others.

Your Journey to Becoming the Go-To Person

Now that you've garnered this rich experience and knowledge, you find a joyous return to being yourself, only more enlightened and grounded. You're like a friendly neighbor who everyone trusts to have the best advice. This role comes with a sweet spot of being able to assist not just customers but friends, family, and neighbors with valuable advice from a place of expertise.

It's like being the local hero who guides people in making the best choices for their homes, and their sacred spaces. Picture yourself as the wise elder in a village, the one who has seen it all, and who has a solution or advice for almost everything. You've become a beacon of trust and reliability, the person people turn to for guidance, transforming everyday problems into moments of learning and growth, a truly rewarding experience.

In this enriched journey of a journeyperson, every day is an opportunity to be that guiding force, bringing comfort and solutions to people's lives, and finding joy and fulfillment in being the helping hand that is always extended, ready to assist and guide. Remember, your role is like that of a seasoned chef who not only knows how to cook a great meal but can also skillfully navigate the chaos of a busy kitchen, turning challenges into opportunities for growth and learning.

A Fulfilling Endeavor

When you step into the world of trades, particularly residential work, you become a part of something much bigger. Picture it akin to being a vital ingredient in a recipe that transforms a house into a home, a place adorned with the personal touches and dreams of its inhabitants. Your role in this transformation is not just a job but a rewarding endeavor, albeit with its fair share of nerve-racking moments.

It's like being a magician with the power to bring long-awaited dreams to fruition, granting homeowners their wishes through renovations and improvements in their personal spaces—from revamping bathrooms and kitchens to constructing dynamic workshops in garages.

Think of it as being the artist who paints canvases, with each stroke bringing a picture to life and bestowing upon it a soul. The sense of accomplishment and the genuine appreciation from homeowners is your masterpiece's applause, the standing ovation for a job well done.

Empowerment Through Skill Acquisition

Besides being a beacon of joy for others, your journeyperson skills equip you with the prowess to craft your living space to echo your heart's desires without draining your pocket. You become a self-sufficient creator, carving out your haven with your own hands, a craftsman with the flair to enhance not only your living space but also to offer your expertise to others, generating additional income beyond your regular job.

The Ascent to Mastery

As years pass, you naturally ponder the trajectory of your growth. It's akin to a scholar with an unquenchable thirst for knowledge, seeking higher education to attain mastery in their field. In the trades sphere, this translates to aspiring to become a master of your trade.

For you, this meant evolving into a master, a role that unfolds an avenue of exciting prospects from spearheading your enterprise, and securing building permits, to possibly mentoring as an inspector. It sets you a notch above the rest in the professional arena, a feat that garners admiration and respect, including from those who watched you grow, like your parents.

This journey is your ode to your parents, a testament to the skills and knowledge they instilled in you, and a beacon encouraging others to relentlessly pursue growth and learning. Remember, your present station is not a final destination but a stepping stone to greater heights. And as I pen this book, I embolden others to embrace the journey of perpetual learning, a journey where every day is a fresh page, a new opportunity to learn, and to grow.

Summary

You delved deep into the meticulous art of being a journeyperson—a role synonymous with precision, detail, and guided learning. This section underlines the importance of developing skills in detailed planning and visualization, whether it's crafting accurate material lists or creating wiring diagrams. This journey is likened to piecing together a complex puzzle, where each entity must find its precise place in a larger framework, a skill that not only paves the way for efficiency and accuracy but potentially opens doors to leadership roles and continuous learning. It fosters a culture of mentorship where the journeyperson transitions from learning to teaching, passing down the garnered knowledge and expertise to the apprentices.

As you progressed further, the chapter broadened its horizon to encompass the essence of teamwork and collaboration in the trade sector. It brought to life the harmonious dance between different trades, illustrating this with the intricate ballet of cooperation between an electrician and a plumber installing a hot water tank. The emphasis here shifts to fostering respect and understanding for fellow tradespeople and honing one's customer service skills, an attribute that holds the power to set one apart in the industry. The narrative promotes a nurturing approach to apprenticeship, fostering a space where learning thrives through positive reinforcement and understanding.

Closing the chapter, you arrived at a reflective juncture where the spotlight is on the rewards and personal fulfillment that come with being a seasoned journeyperson. Here, the role evolves from being just a job to a rewarding vocation that touches lives, brings dreams to fruition, and even lends itself to the comfort and guidance offered to others in personal networks. Moreover, it unveils the road to self-actualization, inspiring individuals to constantly aim higher, potentially aspiring to master their trade and unlock new opportunities that come with it. The chapter closes with an encouraging note, a rallying cry urging individuals to embrace the culture of perpetual learning, viewing their current position as a stepping stone to grander vistas and unexplored territories, nurturing a mindset grounded in growth and learning.

Chapter 8

Project Manager

"Management is doing things right;
leadership is doing the right things."
— Peter Drucker, Management Consultant,
Educator, and Author

8

The Journey from Tools to Leadership

I've shared throughout our story that a trade isn't just a job; it's the start of something bigger, something that can grow as you do. For me, it was a stepping stone that led me from hands-on learning as an electrician to the strategic role of a project manager. It's like being handed a single puzzle piece and discovering it's part of a grander picture. I started with the basics, learning my craft from the ground up, and over time, I transformed those early lessons into a set of problem-solving skills that now define my professional approach.

The Professional Toolkit

When you're skilled with the tools of your trade, you're like a wizard with a wand, expected to make magic happen. That's what it's like on service calls–you're the go-to person, the one who is expected to make things right. And through years of facing these challenges, you develop a knack for it, just like a game-player who learns to anticipate the game's next move. These problem-solving skills are what set you apart, making you a valuable asset not just to your current business but also to potential employers.

Vision and Implementation

Having a career in trades gives you a complete view of how projects come to life. From the very first meeting where ideas are born to the final steps where those ideas take shape, you're there. It's like being both the author and the reader of a story–you know how the plot unfolds because you're the one writing it. The analogy is simple: if the tradesperson is the heart of the project, then the project manager is the mind.

Both are essential, and neither can function well without the other. It's a partnership, a dance where each step is planned and executed with precision and understanding.

The Role of the Project Manager

As a project manager, your role isn't limited to what happens on the ground. Beyond the job site, there's a world of planning and strategy, from drafting designs to finalizing the last piece of paperwork after a job well done.

It's your job to make sure everything stays on track, like a conductor leading an orchestra, ensuring every note is played at the right time and in harmony with the others. This includes the less visible but equally important tasks like handling the budget and ensuring every phase of the project, from conception to close-out, is executed flawlessly.

Orchestrating the Trades

Think of a construction site like an orchestra; each tradesperson is an instrumentalist, and the project manager is the conductor. It's essential for each musician to play their part at the right time to create harmony. In building a home, every trade follows a specific sequence—just like the notes on a musical score.

For example, HVAC technicians lay down their ductwork before an electrician weaves the electrical wires through the structure. If these sequences are out of sync, it can lead to a cacophony of delays and extra costs. It's like trying to bake a cake by adding the frosting before the batter—it just doesn't work.

Guardians of the Project's Heartbeat

Project managers bear the weighty responsibility of approving payments, much like a bank manager overseeing transactions. They must match the work completed with the claims made on invoices, ensuring that every dollar spent reflects actual progress. It's a delicate balance between advancing the project and upholding financial integrity. The project manager stands at the crossroads of protecting the owner's interests and ensuring the contractor profits fairly, much like a tightrope walker balancing high above the ground, moving with precision and care.

Defending the Fortress of Integrity

A project manager also guards the structural integrity of a building, ensuring that the fortress stands strong against the elements and time. They must watch for the smallest leaks, which, like tiny invaders, can undermine the strength of a building's defenses. Overseeing a renovation requires vigilance to ensure no support is removed that could cause the building to falter, akin to removing a cornerstone from an arch. The project manager is the sentinel, tasked with the crucial role of safeguarding the building's integrity from the rooftop to the foundation.

The Visionary's New Horizon

In the role of a project manager, the horizon widens, and responsibility deepens. The insights gained from being on-site, tool in hand, become the foresight to anticipate and mitigate risks before they arise. Just as a captain uses knowledge of the seas to avoid hidden shoals, a project manager leverages on-site experience to navigate projects away from potential pitfalls. Clear, concise thinking that's been sharpened on the job site is what can transform a tradesperson into an outstanding project manager, ready to face the complex, ever-changing landscape of construction management.

Summary

In the journey from skilled tradesperson to project manager, we've discovered that the hands-on experience gained on-site is invaluable when stepping into a role that oversees the full scope of a project. Like learning to play each instrument before conducting an orchestra, a tradesperson's intimate knowledge of their craft ensures a harmonious progression of the construction process. This experience becomes a beacon, guiding projects through the complexities of execution and collaboration, ensuring every piece fits just right.

A project manager's role extends beyond the coordination of tasks; it involves the meticulous oversight of a project's financial heartbeat. They ensure that the rhythm of payments aligns with the pulse of work completed, safeguarding the project's financial health. It's a delicate dance between advancing progress and maintaining integrity, mirroring the precise work of a master artisan ensuring every stroke contributes to the masterpiece's integrity.

In summary, a project manager is the custodian of a project's present and future. They hold the vision that anticipates and prevents structural and financial faults, much like a guardian who foresees potential threats and wards them off before they can cause harm. This foresight, drawn from the well of hands-on experience, equips a tradesperson-turned-project manager with the unique ability to identify and mitigate risks, ensuring the project's success from the ground up.

Chapter 9

Your Exciting Future

*"Success usually comes to those
who are too busy to be looking for it."*
— Henry David Thoreau, American Naturalist,
Essayist, Poet, and Philosopher

9

Your Exciting Future

Picture yourself at the starting line of the most wonderful adventure, ready to step into a world filled with rich experiences and happy moments, made just for you. That's right, it's all out there, waiting for you to grab hold of it! So, let's start this exciting trip into the wonderful world of skilled trades.

A Fire Inside You

Have you ever felt a warm, happy feeling in your heart, pushing you to try something new and big? Well, that's what writing this book feels like. It's like being a chef in a busy kitchen, excited to share a secret recipe with everyone, because it's just too good to keep to yourself.

You see, this book is coming from a place of love and excitement, to help you see the big dreams you can reach. It's like being a helper in a garden, making sure each little plant gets enough water and sunshine to grow tall and beautiful.

Taking It Step by Step

Remember, as you start this special journey, it's all about moving at a pace that feels right for you. Think of it like a friendly race where everyone wins, because the goal isn't just to reach the end, but to enjoy every step along the way.

It took fifty years of learning and growing to understand the secrets to a happy and successful life. It wasn't about becoming a superstar or the richest person; it was about building a life full of respect and joy. It's like building a big, colourful puzzle, one piece at a time, enjoying the picture that comes to life with each piece you add.

So, as we start exploring this path together, remember that it's your path to shape and build, filled with exciting adventures and the joy of learning new things, just like the joy of seeing a small seed grow into a big, strong tree over time.

Taking the Leap

Imagine standing at a crossroad, one path is well-trodden, very familiar, but somewhat plain and predictable. The other is less traveled, but it is brimming with vibrant colours and exciting challenges. That's exactly where I stood before becoming a tradesperson, and choosing the colourful path made all the difference.

Being a Leader and a Problem Solver

Now, think of being a captain of a ship. As a tradesperson, you get to steer your own ship, facing challenges head-on and finding solutions as you go. It's a role for quick thinkers, for people who look at a hurdle and see not a stop sign, but a chance to innovate, to find a new way forward.

Tradespeople are a bit like superheroes, ready to smash through barriers with a determined spirit and a heart full of courage.

They are not satisfied with the ordinary; they crave challenges that test their skills and offer the reward of fulfillment at the end of the day.

Rising Above and Aiming High

You know that feeling when you climb a hill and reach the top, feeling all proud and happy? That's what striving for more feels like in a tradesperson's journey. It's about pushing yourself, just a little bit harder each time, reaching for those stars that seemed too far away, and feeling a rush of happiness with every goal you achieve.

A Rewarding Path of Continuous Growth

Imagine a garden that you tend to every day, watching the plants grow taller and the flowers bloom brighter with your care.

Being a tradesperson is a lot like that garden, constantly growing and blossoming with new opportunities and experiences. It's a career where your mind gets to play and explore, while your hands create wonderful things, bringing joy and fulfillment not just to you, but inspiring others to reach for their dreams too.

Sharing the Treasure Trove of Experience

You know how when you find a really good secret spot, a hidden stream or a beautiful clearing in the woods, you just have to share it with your friends? That's what this book is for me — a way to share the hidden gems and the learning from my journey with you.

The Ups and Downs of a Rewarding Journey

Life is a bit like a roller coaster, isn't it? There are thrilling ups and exciting downs. My journey to becoming a master electrician was a thrilling ride with its share of highs and lows, and I am here to share the reality of that exhilarating journey with you. It's a voyage that has shaped me into who I am, carved out from experiences, both good and bad, each one a valuable lesson that brought me here.

Guiding You Through the Apprenticeship

Think back to when you learned to ride a bike. Remember how someone supported you, steadying the bike until you found your balance? I aim to be that steady hand for you as you navigate the apprenticeship process, offering guidance and sharing wisdom garnered from years of experience, to help you find your own balance and ride confidently on the path of a tradesperson.

Unlocking a World of Opportunities

Imagine finding a key that opens doors to rooms filled with treasures, opportunities, and potentials that you never knew existed. Deciding to take on a trade is like finding that magical key. It empowers you to unlock a future brimming with possibilities, guiding you to become someone you perhaps never imagined, reaching heights you never thought you could. It's an invitation to a life rich with rewards, both big and small, waiting for you to discover and embrace.

Summary

In the early segments of "Your Exciting Future," the underlying impulse steering me to pen down this narrative unravelled, setting a conversational tone that encapsulated the essence of the journey ahead. Drawing upon personal experiences, the text unveiled that embarking on a career in skilled trade is a promise to a path laden with opportunities, open to be explored at one's own pace. Picture it like a guided tour where I am extending a hand to the readers, encouraging them to take the first step in a journey where they not only learn a trade but evolve as individuals, slowly but steadily nurturing their dreams into reality. The spirit of the section is to reassure that one can build a fulfilling life, where every day is a step towards a personal goal, just like patiently building a detailed model, piece by piece.

Venturing further, the narrative shifted to highlight the leadership and problem-solving attributes that often resonate with tradespeople. Through a candid reflection of personal experiences, it showcased a community of vibrant individuals, always ready to face challenges with a can-do attitude. The text is encouraging readers to visualize themselves as the dynamic tradesperson who doesn't settle but carves out a path of extraordinary milestones through hard work and determination. It echoes the spirit of being a go-getter, a pursuer of personal growth, mirroring a mountain climber, eager to reach new heights with every step, showcasing that a career in trades is not just a job but a fulfilling endeavor that offers rich rewards and a chance to constantly evolve.

As the chapter drew to a close, the emphasis was on the essence of sharing learned experiences, likened to passing down a cherished recipe through generations. It reiterated that the journey as a tradesperson is not just about personal growth but sharing that growth and knowledge with others. It is about teaching, guiding budding apprentices, and helping them appreciate the rewards that a career in trades can bestow. This section is a warm invitation, encouraging readers to envisage the transformative power a career in trades holds, empowering them to transform into someone they never imagined, nurturing a spirit akin to a seasoned gardener, encouraging a new sapling to grow, fostering it with knowledge and experience. It portrays the trades career as a cycle of learning, growing, and sharing, a fulfilling circle of professional life.

Chapter 10

Sky is the Limit

"The sky is not the limit; your mind is."
— Marilyn Monroe, American Actress, Model, and Singer

10

Dream Big, but Dream Smart

In a world where you are the master of your ship, remember, no dream is too big, it's only the timelines that can sometimes be a bit tight. Imagine you are crafting the most intricate sandcastle on the beach. Sometimes, the tide might come in faster than you anticipate. But that shouldn't stop you from dreaming or trying, it just means sometimes you need a bit more time.

The Unique Snowflake in You

Picture yourself as a unique snowflake amidst a sky full of them, each having its distinct pattern and trajectory. Just like that, you carry a uniqueness that is utterly yours. In your journey, it's vital to recognize and applaud your uniqueness, just as you would marvel at a lone beautiful snowflake drifting down from the sky. Cherish your individuality and allow it to shine in the career path you carve out for yourself.

Listing Your Triumphs

Think about a time when you were a child, keeping a keen record of your little wins; maybe it was a star on a chart, or a sticker in a book. Now, as an adult, foster that childlike enthusiasm by keeping a list of your triumphs and victories. This isn't just a trip down memory lane; it's your personal scoreboard, a testament to your capabilities, always reminding you of your strengths when doubts try to creep in.

Stepping Stones in Your Career

Consider your career as a series of stepping stones across a lively stream. Some stones might be a bit shaky, some quite firm, and some leading you to paths you didn't envision initially. Remember, every step you take is a chance to learn, grow, and perhaps step onto a path more exciting and fulfilling than you initially imagined.

The Infectious Nature of Success

As you forge ahead, you will notice that success isn't just a personal joy; it's infectious, encouraging others around you to strive for their peaks as well. Imagine your career as a blossoming garden, where your growth and blooming flowers inspire others to grow and bloom beautifully too, creating a garden vibrant with colours and fragrances.

Sending Out Positive Energies

As you stride further, be conscious of the energies you are sending out into the universe. Picture it as a boomerang; what you send out will return to you. Nurturing a clear vision and increasing your visibility are like sending out a boomerang with a clear goal, ensuring it returns with the desired outcome.

Self-Belief: Your Strongest Companion

There will be moments when you feel like a solitary tree in a desert, holding onto the belief in your dreams when no one else does. In those moments, stand tall, dig deep, and hold onto your visions, for only you have the ultimate clarity and focus on what you want, and only you can bring your dreams to fruition.

Interlacing Your Interests with Your Career

As you embark further, remember to weave in your interests into your career tapestry. It's like mixing your favorite colours while painting, creating a masterpiece that is both pleasing and uniquely yours, a career where your interests don't just stay hobbies but become a fulfilling part of your daily life.

Unleashing Your Potential

Lastly, be your best judge to determine your conducive environment that maximizes your skills. Envision yourself as a plant choosing the right type of soil and the right amount of sunshine to grow into the tallest, strongest tree in the forest. Remember, the sky's the limit, and it's you who sets the boundaries for your growth. Embrace your potential, for your journey upwards is only just beginning.

Becoming a Beacon of Knowledge

As you grow in your trade, a new horizon opens up where you become a guiding light for others, a teacher perhaps. Remember those first days when you were learning to ride a bicycle, and there was someone there to hold the bike steady? Now, it's your turn to be that steadying hand, helping others to find their balance and start pedaling in the world of trades.

Stepping into the Shoes of an Inspector

As time moves forward, just like a seasoned chef can tell a good dish from a bad one with just a simple taste, you too develop a keen eye, capable of inspecting and evaluating other tradespersons' work. You become like a wise old tree, able to offer shelter and guidance with your deep-rooted knowledge and expansive canopy of experience.

The Pathway to Becoming an Estimator

Now imagine yourself holding a magical crystal ball, using your learned skills to estimate costs and give companies an accurate picture of a project's financial landscape. It's a role where your expertise meets foresight, much like a captain steering a ship safely through a storm, using both knowledge of the sea and understanding of the ship's strengths.

Embarking on a Business Adventure

Next, visualize opening the doors to your own contracting business. It's like building your own treehouse, deciding on its size, its features, and who gets to come in. Here, the sky is the limit. You decide whether your business is a cozy hut or a sprawling mansion, tailoring it perfectly to match your vision and ambition.

Leadership and Greatness

Owning a business isn't just about financial rewards; it's about stepping into a role of responsibility, leadership, and even greatness. Think back to your favorite storybook hero or heroine growing up—now, you are stepping into a similar role, leading with honesty and striving to achieve your carefully cultivated dreams.

A Journey of Continuous Growth

Remember, every day is a school day. With every interaction, you find yourself learning, earning, and yearning for more. It's a dynamic dance where you are constantly evolving, much like a river that never stops flowing, carving new paths and discovering unseen vistas.

A Service of Mastery

As you carve your niche, becoming a master in your field, people begin to appreciate your service, showering you with respect and admiration. It's a warm feeling, akin to receiving a hearty applause after a well-played game, acknowledging your hard work, dedication, and expertise. Through your journey, you morph from a budding apprentice to a respected master, offering essential services, much like a diligent gardener nurturing seeds into full-grown, flourishing plants that everyone admires and appreciates.

Summary of All Chapters

Dear Reader, as a helping hand to you, I am now summarizing briefly each chapter of my book.

In the first half of the book, you undertook an enlightening journey where you were empowered to actively pursue a fulfilling career in skilled trades. The initial chapters are a potent guide aimed at you, if you are ready to immerse yourself in an apprenticeship, guiding you through the path to finding a job that you love and nurturing your skill set to foster a rewarding future.

Chapter 1, aptly titled "Decide," lays down the foundational philosophy guiding your pursuit as an apprenticeship in skilled trades. It evokes your passion, emphasizing hands-on learning and encouraging you to be steadfast in seeking a profession that truly satisfies your spirit. It urges you to envision a future enriched through tangible experiences, setting the stage for a fulfilling journey through the world of skilled trades.

Chapter 2 delves into the logistics of navigating your apprenticeship period. It explores the interdependence of theory and practical knowledge, shedding light on the 'amperage of your apprenticeship,' a term coined to describe the essence of personalized learning speeds during apprenticeship. This chapter encourages you to pace yourself, understanding and embracing the highs and lows of your journey, all while holding the reins of your educational advancements firmly in your hands.

As you venture into Chapter 3, you witness a compelling portrayal of the skilled trades sector as a harmonious ground that welcomes diversity with open arms. It paints a vivid picture of an industry ready to shatter stereotypes and encourage you to forge your unique path, underlining the boundless opportunities available in this sector. This chapter is an open invitation for you to find your niche in this expansive and inclusive landscape, encouraging you to carve out a fulfilling career in a domain as vibrant and diverse as a rainbow.

Chapter 4 marks a significant turn in the narrative as it focuses on the rising opportunities for women in the skilled trades sector. It demolishes outdated gender-related stereotypes, emphasizing the evolving role of women in this field. It not only encourages women to see themselves as an integral part of this industry but also as leaders, guiding the narrative towards inclusivity and diversity. The Canadian government's role in fostering gender diversity through various initiatives forms a crucial part of this chapter, urging women to seize the myriad opportunities available in the sector.

Chapter 5 expands the horizon further, emphasizing the wealth of opportunities available in Canada for new Canadians, including immigrants and women. It offers a beacon of hope, providing essential guidance on how to navigate the skilled trades sector in Canada, right from acknowledging foreign qualifications to learning English or French to facilitate better integration into the Canadian workforce. The chapter portrays Canada as a land of opportunities, with the skilled trades sector standing as a pillar supporting the dreams and aspirations of new Canadians, promising not just financial stability but a chance to forge a fulfilling career.

In conclusion, the first half of the book stands as a powerful testimony to the rich, diverse, and ever-evolving landscape of skilled trades. Through vivid imagery and inspiring narratives, it guides you through the initial yet crucial steps of embarking on an apprenticeship journey. It paints a canvas of opportunities, urging you to embrace your unique skills and forge paths adorned with perseverance, creativity, and individuality. It is more than just a guide; it is a beacon illuminating the path to a fulfilling career in the skilled trades, a path characterized by self-discovery, inclusivity, and boundless opportunities. It is a hearty call to you in any walk of life to write your own apprenticeship story with resilience.

In the second part of the book, you walk through the rich and evolving journey of someone learning and growing in the skilled trades profession over four reflective chapters. From a beginner to a skilled expert, you witness the milestones of a fulfilling career pathway.

In Chapter 6, your journey as an apprenticeship begins with a mix of fear and growing self-confidence. I share my personal experience, emphasizing the critical role of mentors and a supportive learning environment. Through my story, you understand the apprenticeship not just as a learning period but a time of personal growth where a newbie transforms into a valuable team member.

Chapter 7 takes you deeper into the life of a journeyperson, where careful planning and foresight become essential tools. Here, you learn about the importance of teamwork and collaboration in the trade sector, promoting a respectful and understanding work culture. The chapter beautifully describes the journey from learning to teaching, encouraging continuous learning and growth.

In Chapter 8, the perspective broadens to showcase the wide range of opportunities available in the skilled trades. I encourage you to start with a strong foundation, likening the career progression to a sapling growing into a strong tree. The focus shifts to the significance of collaboration and understanding among team members to achieve successful projects. Towards the end, there is a thoughtful discussion about the crucial roles of both project managers and skilled tradespeople, encouraging you to think about the important contributions of each role in a project.

Chapter 9 welcomes you to a world full of unexplored paths and opportunities in the skilled trades profession. It emphasizes individual growth that comes with the profession, encouraging you to envision yourself growing and evolving in the field. Towards the end of the chapter, the focus is on sharing knowledge and experience, encouraging newcomers to grow and fostering a fulfilling cycle of learning and teaching in the profession.

In Chapter 10, you continue to follow the journey of learning a skilled trade from start to mastery. Building on ideas from earlier chapters, this part looks at the bigger roles you can take on as you get better and more experienced in your job. It talks about the steps to becoming a leader in the field or maybe even starting your own business. You can expect to hear more personal stories and advice about moving up in a skilled trade career. This chapter then encourages you to keep learning and growing, not just for yourself but to help others in your community too. This chapter aims to give a full picture of the many opportunities available in a skilled trades career, showing it's not just a job, but a path that can lead to a satisfying and rewarding life.

Across these chapters, the narrative not only describes a career path but fosters a deep understanding and appreciation for the skilled trades profession, depicting it as a fulfilling and rewarding journey. It encourages you to envision a career built on continuous growth, collaboration, and the joy of mastering a skill while emphasizing the important role of mentorship in this field.

Enjoy your new life in the skilled trades.

See you on the job site.

About The Author

J ason Mullen lives with his now-teen children, Meraina (18) and Quin (15).

Jason is a Master Electrician in the Province of Ontario and he loves this trade. His current title is Project Manager for Peel District School Board. But, recently, his love has extended to helping young adults discover the world of trades as an excellent and valuable way of life. He holds seminars for corporations, school boards and trade schools, helping those organizations guide audience members to consider the trades.

You may contact Jason at
success@TransformationByTrade.com to book him
as a speaker or a private coach.